THIS JOURNAL BELONGS TO:

___

Made in United States
Orlando, FL
22 May 2022

18084949R00111